THE COLOR AFTER GREEN

poems by

H. R. Spencer

Finishing Line Press
Georgetown, Kentucky

THE COLOR
AFTER GREEN

ACKNOWLEDGMENTS

"Instructions for Kayaking" (as "Lake Murray Journal") was in *The Sense of the Midlands;* "The Deer Keeper," in *Fall Lines;* "Writing on Calendar: Directions to Jan's Place" was published in *The South Carolina Collection;* "Ice Storm" and "The Dolphin" were in *The Failure of Magic;* ". . . each year," "It Is Dangerous Work to Winter Here," "Transparencies," "Letting Go," and "Georgia O'Keeffe Talks About Her Paintings, 1. The Red Poppy" were in *What the Body Knows.*

Publisher: Leah Maines
Editor: Christen Kincaid
Cover Art: H. R. Spencer
Author Photo: Jordan Spencer
Cover Design: Leah Huete

Printed in the USA on acid-free paper.
Order online: www.finishinglinepress.com
also available on amazon.com

Author inquiries and mail orders:
Finishing Line Press
P. O. Box 1626
Georgetown, Kentucky 40324
U. S. A.

Table of Contents

Part IV.

For Jordan and Colin

What my [grandchildren] learn of the sea
of the summer thunders
of the riddles that hide in the curve of spring
[they] will learn in my twilights

Audre Lorde,
"What My Child learns of the Sea"

I.

the brief air the vanishing green. . .
now we have only the words we remember
to say to each other. . .

W. S. Merwin,
"Before Us"

The Deer Keeper

The construction site edges closer.
They adapt. Hemmed in
browsing forb, vines, woody stems
shy trespassers they come closer
dine at our ornamental table
taking first the hostas
then daylilies and hydrangeas
leaving alone the lantana
the cannas and angelonia.

•

The small isthmus traps her here
she gives birth
spindly-legged, a head taller
than neighborhood dogs
her twin fawns frolic in the grass.
When she sees our puppy whining
through the window
she lowers her ears
stares directly at him
hair raised on the back of her neck
stomping the ground one hoof at a time
moving the fawns to safety.

•

Our doe returns
usually late afternoons
walks the property line
between mine and my neighbor's yards.
There are no fences
though she still walks
with this tentative shyness
as if there were some unconscious boundary
She's calm. We keep the dog shut away.

•

Daily, a ritual now
we watch each other watch each other
through glass
through the kitchen window
nervously, both of us trying not to move,
neither of us yet quite at ease,
neither of us quite appreciating this new connection.

•

Now no sightings now for five days,
before that only the lone doe—no fawns—on Tuesday
lingering cautiously, more vigilant,
too often only the undiluted sound of bulldozers
skimming across vacated forests.

•

Three coyotes were spotted again
crossing the road together this morning.

•

At noon, dark shadows glide across the grass
leaping over the smaller brush
glancing sideways off the pines
silhouettes, broad wingtips
notched into five black fingers.
There are three at first, then four and five
crossing in narrowing circles
floating closer, then rising on updrafts
then dropping finally
until they disappear down behind the treeline.

Dust

So much studiously observed,
now more, these corals, these great sea fans
                    dying off Antigua and St. John,

and knowledge it is only
in brown grit that whirls
from its dry bowl in Africa,

a poison crossing the Atlantic,
a yellow cloud spotted overhead by satellite.
                    Where it salts the Caribbean

a sample sifts into our cone filter,
dust that carries the thready aspergillus,
innocuous, a soil fungus everywhere

yet somehow its conveyance toxic
among these friable polyps, their immune response
                    breathtakingly purple even underwater,

an unsuccessful response. It is possible
a core drilled now into this reef gives us a text,
would read for us which were the drought years below the Sahara,

would reveal how everything is connected, a chain,
life being how we manage the particulars.
                    Until now, without clear reason,

these deaths had seemed surrounding and obscure,
the sea's lacy needlework
falling victim mysteriously. Only now, underwater,

where we can watch the fans sway, their incredible undulations
straining plankton from the current, do we know
                    how this brown death settles around them.

It Fell Not

That summer we waited for the crowd to leave Bar Harbor,
Arriving after even the whales and osprey have gone,
The slue-footed lobster decamped for deeper water.

Your windowsill at the hundred-year-old Clairemont
hosted an exquisite nautilus. Unroofed, its rooms opened
to air out their mollusc musk. It belonged

more to an architect's rendering than to life, that cousin
to the chimeric squid, flashing its neon unseen
in an unseen sea. A blustery, chill, October sea wind

had settled in. When we shoved off toward Little Cranberry
swarms of mackerel frenzied off the bow rail
like twisted bracelets. A white gold. In the background trees

lay hidden in the broken fog that covered Isle
au Haut. Behind the converted mailboat's stiff churn
lobsterers steadied by their stern sails,

steered windward like ducks. In heavy seas our boat turned
leeward toward Sutton Island's calm. There the osprey nest stood alone
on bare rock. Each spring's generations of great birds returned

here. Their home, erected biblically on stone,
had stood for sixty years, every osprey pair
adding to its height, now twenty feet. Each twig bareboned,

it survived when floods came, and *when the rare
winds blew and beat upon the house . . . it fell not,*
its palimpsest of un-wordy woven sticks its own truth in the ripe air.

It Is Dangerous Work to Winter Here

All night from our window, New England's stout,
sore-thumbed lighthouses massage the dark.
This far north the ocean seems more curved.
"Depression would be too easy here," you say.
"no subterfuge. People bound so closely together.
They see too much of each other. Long nights,
and cold. Marriages stretch to the breaking point."
Conversations we overhear leaden like glass,
Nerves rubbed together like two sticks, charred.
It's nearly midnight when we leave the restaurant,
search for a coin laundry, listen absently
to news of the day. Under the Atlantic's
severe gray two more urchin divers have died.
"The market rate, published this morning," I comment,
"is less than a dollar a pound." Their bodies,
brought up this afternoon, lie in a row on trays,
as sorrowfully as cod.

Birds of America

O' winter war,
And thro' the drift,
Ilk happing bird, wee, helpless thing!
What comes o' thee?
Where wilt thou cow'r thy chittering wing
An' close thy e'e?
—Robert Burns

My mockingbirds, whose music delighted me by the hour,
And one, to whom I gave a name, perched on my writing table
And followed me up the stairs when I retired to nap.
They flew about the White House singing Scottish ditties,
Said to be my constant companions during the solitudes of those hours.
True enough, they were my only pleasure after Mrs. Jefferson died
And helped to offset my dimnishing love for High Office.

Long retired now, I note each Spring appearances at Monticello
Of Meadowlarks and Martins, Redbreasts and Whippoorwills,
And along the lowland rivers those fiendish Paraquets from Carolina.
Here, purple Martins are the true wellcomers of Spring, having roosted
Together in hollow trees in full torpor over our coldest winter months,
An explanation which my good friend Chastellux adamantly disputes.
At night we read the Scotsman Burn's poetry together in the fire's glow
And he expounds his beliefs on those migrations of birds,
His thoughts being similar to those of most Europeans
That these birds, in fact, migrate annually, a point of view
Which I find irreconcilable with my own evidence, for I have seen
Proof, even, that house swallows lie at the bottoms of rivers
During winter months and emerge only in April to our delight.

Most recently I have come upon the paintings from young Audubon,
An instructor he is at Jefferson College. I much admire his work
And accord him well both as painter and ornithologist,
For he has himself observed how the Paraquets, too, in winter
Do not fly south, but cluster together by thousands in rotted trunks
Of sycamores. This he dutifully recorded in December
along the Ohio River, and I would have added to my own observations
and hastened to describe for Chastellux at our last meeting.

Environmental Studies

Beside the house
long-leafed Virginia pines
ate up the raw red hillside
where morning glories
and wild hibiscus
grew down to the water
and hemstitch tracks from
blue herons were left to shiver
in the gooey mud

vegetation choked the pond,
invasive grasses
as dense as sea kelp.
We drained the water
to kill the grass
killed everything else.
Only turtles tucked
into the greenish muck
would wait us out
and small gnats
whose day-long lives
replenished
on exposed bottoms

Refilled by rain
water trickled over the spillway.
Glassy nymphs of eels
scaled its sheer walls
clinging to algae tufts
and mortar joint,
and the nuisance plants
came back. We scattered bags of fertilizer
over the water
hoping algae would
grow so fast and block the light
enough to smother unwanted elodia,
but this also failed

and oxygen enough for fish
was gone.
One by one the turtles
sunk each floating
corpse of bass or bream,
left visible only the murky blue-green
bloom of algae.

2,3,7,8, tetrachlorodibenzo-para-dioxin

We were boys when the eelgrass died
no idea why, maybe only now,
in retrospect understood as suspended silt
farm run-off, blocking sunlight
until the grass thinned markedly, turned brown
broke away from the sandy bottom
clumps of it washing ashore.

The blue crabs we depended on
for summer's spending money
disappeared
soft-shelled hardest to find
the few that remained burrowing themselves
almost invisibly in the soft mud
only black eyestalks
protruding while their shells hardened

With luck, we netted a few molts, *busters*,
halfway through their shedding,
they could only swim awkwardly,
could not dig easily into the river bottom
nicking their claws
to keep others safe in the crab box

We were ignorant then, never understood
our pitifully small catch
had never heard of dioxin
how it could kill the larvae.
We could not spell *harbinger*
could not fathom the cancer
that grew inside the livers of workers
handling the pesticide upriver
could not imagine
how it would settle in the soft ooze
at the bottom of the channel
how fifty years later its poison
barely altered, would still sit there.

Eco-Travel

The trip is gruelling
the thrill of eco-touring diminishing
with the drudgery of five-hour bus rides
over rock roads that sheer off into space,
peculiar toileting protocols,
even with the continuous buffet lines
trumpeting authentic Costa Rican fare
that become the same one line after another
as if we were home comparing hamburgers
at fast food chains.

Tortuqureo is reachable
only in a cramped water taxi.
In the drying river we have to change seats
shift our weight to one side or the other
when the driver employs a pole to shove us free,
quarrelsome crocodiles quarantined
onto mud banks,
the rainless rainforest warming,
Earth's habitable zone narrowing.

Hovering over us, perfectly-adapted sloths
hang like large fruits in umbrella trees.
Four-foot head-to-toe, blue-faced iguanas,
pre-historic, are motionless in the grass.
Scarlet macaws dazzle
Montezuma orioles balance
perched on bare branches in the water,
even our migratory North American
night herons settling here for the winter.

At night, the howler monkeys are restless
hope rises momentarily, then only dry thunder.

At dawn, dour, unresponsive,
the coconut man from Tortuguero
crosses back and forth in front of our cabin

each time pushing the deep mason's wheelbarrow
filled with his morning's collection

Still no rain. You purchase a turtle carved
from a palm seed, carry it home.

The Balance of Nature

The text we taught ourselves
had it wrong
nature's balance less certain
more imperfect
not simply predator-prey
in some refined dance
for each to survive
in sufficient numbers,
ideas now out of whack
questioned now
Isle Royale a case in point
survival of the wolf tribe
being partly a matter of luck,
partly dependent
on the personalities of leaders
how cautious, how intelligent,
how strong or brave or willing
to defend their territory,
and less likely, a mutation
that unlocks recessive genes.
Our reintroductions are beautiful to watch,
but their elegant trophic cascades
fraught with unpredictables
variables here or there
not anticipated

In Yellowstone
its wolf-elk-aspen model strains
jarred askew when grizzlies,
driven by hunger, alter their diet,
replace spawning cutthroat trout,
(those trout taken
by deeper-water lake trout
larger, voracious, thriving non-natives)
so bears, unwilling to relocate
harvest the newborn elk instead
out-competing the wolf,

wolves themselves
reintroduced only two decades ago,
so that over time one or more species
is destined to get the upper hand
to shift the *balance*
the teeter board of nature
rising and dipping wildly,
out of our control.

If we wanted to keep it simple,
how naive we were, as even now
guided by rangers' hands
electric shocks target, newly-hatched,
the lake trout fry
and cutthroat numbers slowly return.

Blindness: Two Parables

1. The Parable of the Blind Cave Fish

Deep in a cave in the North Carolina Mountains, our guide extinguishes his lantern. He tells us that no matter how long we remain standing there that our eyes will never adapt to the dark, and not a single scintilla of light will ever touch or stimulate our retinas, and in a short time we will go blind. Carefully, with his light he points to where the trout are swimming, the underground stream that runs slowly beside us. We are not allowed to shine our own flashlights in their direction. Though they are for all intents completely blind, any sudden bright light, he believes, would still cause confusion, disorient them. They would never, he tells us, be able to recover their sight should they emerge from the cave to live in sunlight. Nonetheless, he adds hopefully, if one blind fish happens to mate with another trout living outside, at least a portion of their offspring would be able to see.

2. The Parable of the Barnacle

The young barnacle, our guide tells us, leaves the early protective care of the parent and enters a new phase in their life. Free-swimming, the microscopic cyprid in time develops a pair of fully-functioning eyes. In this stage it consciously searches for a hard surface, a rock, a piling, or a large shell, on which to establish an adult home. Such a home will last for the rest of its life. But using this vision so adroitly the young barnacle searches not for just a suitable lodging, but also one where others have already settled, a necessity if it is ever to mate. When a site is chosen, the maturing barnacle attaches head first, its eyes facing toward the rock. It begins to construct a hard shell, one increasingly calcified over time that serves to protect what is most fragile and vulnerable in its life. Sight is extinguished. Soon the eyes atrophy and completely vanish. From that point forward, our guide says, the barnacle will lie on its back, its feet pointed up, blind, unable to ever change positions again, immobile for the remainder of its life. It is an oddity of the modern world, he tells us sadly, that the warming earth bathes the young cyprids in intolerable amounts of light, ultraviolet light, and that the unwanted light damages their eyes to the point that they are unable see well enough to locate suitable sites where other barnacles have already attached and they have lost any chance to mate.

. . . no swirling current

here, twice the size of Texas,
only the prevailing westerlies
that target our cove
today's largess light
only a 2 liter soda bottle
telltale label sun-faded
and shredded, a child's
water noodle bobbing
in the gentle onrush
debris that includes
the styrofoam top
to someone's fishing cooler
a red-and-white float
still attached to a rat's nest
tangle of fishing line
the shattered tip of
someone's kayak paddle
wire mesh bait bucket
with drowned crickets
a split piece of decking
storm-torn from a floating dock
a hank of rope, a "jitterbug—"
or at least what we used
call a jitterbug—lure
and two beer cans, one crushed,
yet no swirling current here
twice the size of Texas.

The Color After Green

I will know how green is spelled
when it is not green
                    —W.S. Merwin, "Tracing the Letters"

Last night the shrill frogs' chorale
was more like tinnitus
than tinnitus itself, indistinguishable
from the dreaming mind's meandering.
This morning bumblebees,
hundreds cover the bottlebrush.
All is not well.
It is early May. Ninety degrees.
Geese are punished into a listless shade.
A purposeful heron stalks a bream
in slow motion at the water's edge.
Spring's ducklings, even mayflies
have yet to appear. Song birds,
finches and chickadees,
no longer at the feeder, summer further north.

I'm up at seven, house painting early
to avoid the heat. *Taupe*, the dealer calls it,
but really green with a twist of brown.
Leaves, too, brown along their edges
and the lakebed already
starts to show through like an old sore.
Another summer coming like the last—
a grim test of survival.

The nights are stifling. At three a.m.
the frogs, in unison, go suddenly silent.

II.

Whoever spoke to me first—
rock, wind, bird, or fir—whoever broke
the membrane of silence. . .

Gyorgyi Voros
"Forest Orison"

Instructions for Kayaking

Morning

step down cautiously
single foot first, center of gravity low
as not to disturb the water
lapping underneath

observe the lake, quicksilver
broad, slow swells
sweep bank the bank
across the cove

listen. absolute stillness
nothing moves but sound
birds, unseen, dart noisily tree to tree
in the sharp air

push out slowly, quietly
try not to shatter the water
its glass moment.
feather the paddle to gain air

slip silently into fog.
the horizon, losing traction, crimps beneath the keel.
a single row of pines
rappels against the granite sky

there, beneath the water the gaze of a fish
the obligation of a stone.
Listen obliquely
to the osprey's cries of alarm

Afternoon

note how water cannot distinguish
the paddles' dimpled symmetries
from the water strider's

purposeful scurrying

near the shore a green anole
stretches on a dry buttonbush
its throaty red luminescence
capturing sunlight

under a clabbered sky
a Brownian flight
of mayflies
anchors a river birch

flower-heads of mimosa
float down
pirouette in the swirling air
onto a shimmering stage

shorten your stroke
glide slowly
inside the willow's green trellis
a water snake curls on rough bark

look down in the clear water
hollowed out, closely-guarded
a bream bed has stirred up
a trove of chalky, broken clamshells

a thin rain
pricks the skin of the cove
circles widen,
disappear

Evening

feel the wind ripen,
streamers of foam flash across the cove
slither like snakeheads

into riprap

migratory martins
bob and weave
skim across the water
first three, then a dozen, then uncountable

through a narrow opening
watch an early moon
visible through the tall pines
its archetypal resistance to darkness

flints of stars
strike across the night's cold steel
sparks dance
helter-skelter in the black water

hauled up, overturned
the empty kayak
squats like a disgruntled terrapin
trailing sinewy lake water

. . . to paint clouds

as bodies of water
no longer puffs of cotton, spun confections
but eddies, currents, great sweeping tides
brown sea-trout migrating through their cataracts
cloudfish born in those waters
swimming there
leaping after venturesome dragonflies
hovering over cloudponds

to paint them with more than the color of battleships
more than the vacuous white absence of color
but sea-green, viridian, ochre
the blush of pomegranate, orange
a full palate suspended above a pale earth
a noisy roiling of clouds
an incendiary alizarin
a fugitive rose madder, impermanent
ceding to the earth
patterns crocheted light
wobbling against Prussian blue shadow

the sky as liquid
enormous bellows of water panting
breathless
the earth floating beneath it
the earth born out of this cloudwomb

Georgia O'Keeffe Talks About Her Paintings

1. The Red Poppy

"My first memory is of red."

Is it possible I could be so struck by red,
enough to sacrifice everything to paint one flower,
a flower that will be gone by morning, by morning only
a bruised capsule of color inert on the greenhouse floor?

Could I as much as that ruby-throated bird
be so captivated by the edgy geography
displayed inside the red poppy, double-flowering,
a carmine mirror held up in answer to its absent voice?

Is it possible I could also be struck by such color,
struck dumb so that like that bird I could hover
inches from an observing face, unnoticed? Is it possible
that within my own whir of unstoppable wings beating

the vermilion gouache of the flower could displace
everything? Could the color red do this?

2. The Black Iris

Those white trumpets flowered first, exposing memory:
the early years, the total contentment.
Petals touched the milky rim of innocence
on such a grand scale that only I could see.

Then, ruby-striated, the pulpit flowers were drawn
into me. They were dark, angular as *City Night*,
its twirling, shell-burst stars, enigmatic, a brightness
within darkness. I painted: always alone, silent, withdrawn

until, at last, the black iris opened me.
Pink-tongued, it awakened a rapturousness,
surprising me with its *un-paintable clear consciousness.*

Overpowered, I wanted to undress and pull it inside me.

I wanted history to know that I was a source,
that I explored what only a woman could explore.

The Necessity of Art

*The last Carolina Parakeet died in February, 1918
in captivity at the Cincinnati Zoo*

My Dear Friend Bachman,

Your letters, John, are all the more dear
to me now. Daytimes so often I am morose,
filled with longing to escape, though
it would seem there is no reason why.

My studio alone is full of such exotic birds,
specimens so carefully preserved,
and from my window elk and fox return
nightly, and I can witness buffalo giving birth.

Still, my mind wanders. I imagine those rivers,
roads I travelled for so many years. I no longer paint.
In the mid-range my eyesight has deteriorated.
Not enough remains to draw with any authority.

I live in the past, my mind loitering,
as it were, on old favorites, paintings of birds
which seem so fresh as though finished only a fortnight
ago. Those *paraquets*, for example, remain vivid

in my mind, their emerald feathers, such dazzle
I had no choice but to paint with a bright-green malachite,
my watercolors layered over pastel to capture
their brightness. Wings shaded with Prussian blue,

so many washes they were almost black. I loved
the lemony yellow of their heads, the masks
of carmine, dagger-shaped from the beak backward
to encircle the eye. I know I need not describe

all this to you. At my first sight of them,
it was extraordinary. Their numbers were so great
they would fill the sky. They had lived

harmlessly, a sparse diet, mostly fruit from cockleburs.

Farmers hated the cockleburs. They saw them
as only noxious impediments to clearing
and planting, burs you could hardly pull
from clothing or would mat their horses' tails

to the point the flowing skirts of those animals
had to be bobbed. They pulled them from the ground
by their roots, and the paraquets began instead
to harvest the farmers' unripe fruit, immature nuts,

kernels of grain. With my own eyes
I saw them pluck every apple from a tree
enough to ruin an entire crop.
But their demise, of that you know well enough,

for when the farmer killed a single bird
the others would fly up in alarm, then circle
and return and hover closely about
their dead member. This flocking behavior,

they call it, would make certain that with his
next aim the husbandman would kill not one,
but a large number with a single shot
and little ammunition used. In such easy manner

I gathered a basketful of birds to use as specimens
from which to make my graphite studies.
Seven birds were needed where I posed them
pinned in various attitudes to a stout board

What has happened, Bachman, to those fair creatures?
Their numbers were declined by half before
I finished my painting, and half again
or more by now, so much so I fear

my paintings might be all that will remain to remind
my own grandchildren, my meticulous engravings
serving as tombstones for these remarkable birds. This causes
much sorrow in my last years, for truly, I write,

To hunt, to kill without necessity is murder.

              Your most grateful friend,
              J. J. Audubon

. . . at the Saltbox Gallery,

back from the washateria, the morning's basket full,
Tom and Peter, Petite Riviere's
two ex-pat artists up from Vermont
open their studio to *guests.*
Brushes lifting pigments from their full palettes
have cross-pollinated every stick of furniture,
riotous chairs, benches covered with pure swaths of color
as bright as any Shelburne quilt. On the gallery's walls
a dozen folk art Atlantic cod hang,
four feet mouth-to-tail.
I select: *Return of the Transatlantic Cod Balloon,*
a calico dirigible hanging airborne over
Lunnenburg's five-trinket waterfront
where, two-masted, the schooner-rigged,
Bluenose II sets out from harbor.

The Atlantic cod here are gone now.
Inshore, they bring in allowable numbers
of haddock, "sustainable" being the catchword,
while farther out the mega-trawlers
dump their unlicensed bycatch
as so much discardable debris,
this island where the loyalist Tories
fled after Independence was declared,
then fled again when disinterested King George
closed his larder and stranded them
hungry and destitute with winter coming.
From the road next to our rented cottage
the cemetery runs up a hill. Their backs to the ocean,
all the inscriptions face shoreward
so that widows can watch the sea as they read the graves.

Hunger closes in again, fish stocks dropping,
boats idled, and even lobster gathered
on a schedule rotating village port to village port.
The cod's balloon likeness hangs at home
as if its colors could cast a spell of magic.

. . . the blue

heron, impertinent,
sticks his landing
on the Bimini top
of our boat,
not a perch for hunting,
but merely
to demonstrate status
in his shoreside habitat.
Hungry later,
he will drop down
to grovel
among shallows
a beak's depth,
pick an unlucky bream
struck
with a dizzying thrust,
flipped up like a flapjack
to aim it
fin-safe, head-first
into his gullet,
swallowing slowly,
grappling fifteen minutes
with the ungainly bulge
tucked into
an otherwise graceful neck,
satisfied,
simply wanders
in the light ripples
a posing master
over his domain.

The Naturalists

"Mallards mate for life," I told her.
Our kayak glided across the cove.
"I know," she answered,
That day, though, we witnessed something other
even among waterfowl.
A single green-headed drake
beat back another, a rival
and seized him by the neck
held him underwater
but that second male, when free,
circled the lake, returned
and mounted the helpless female
with a brutish ferosity.
The cockhold mate was stunned.

"Is love always something personal?" she asked,
"something shared," the tension there in her voice,
thrusting her paddle forward,
its spooned curette
stripping the fleshy water
from the kayak's skin,
the prow scattering the ducks,
their wings beating like paddles against the water.

We watched it happen like that
four straight days, the intruder returning
to assault the drab-colored duck
and each night she moved further from me
across the bed, flat and wide as a small pond,
the sheets rippling against the headboard
in small waves when I moved after her.

"I have been dreaming," she told me,
holding her hand in a *back-off* warning "of that duck,
the awfulness of the whole thing
day after day like this,"
and accused me of dreaming the dream of drakes.

"Which drake?" I chided her,
"The one failing to protect his lover, or the other."
"The latter," she answered defiantly
as though it must be true,
tying herself into a knot
at the far edge of the mattress.

"I dream," I told her,
"that we could make love dropping over the falls
in a barrel, or underwater, or sky diving
like eagles falling a thousand feet in one embrace,"
keeping silent
that I knew I also saw in my sleep that mallard drake,
still unrepentant, his bilious green head
luminescent in the dark,
leaving only strained metaphors taken from nature,
our anthropomorphic musings on ducks,
to break our silence.

Writing on Calendar:
Directions to Jan's Place

out of Sonoma
cross the free grange
over cattle guards
past shingleless barn
(sunlit in waffle patches
on ivy floor)
down to Shell Beach
hand over hand along slippery rock
hunt for bearded mussels
in the *"un-r'd"* season
in pools of rock-caught urchin, anemone
fill galvanized bucket

at night they will open
like sweet thighs
moved by the butter's warm aphrodisia

Fault Lines

Broad plates slide under us
as wide as oceans.
The Earth is liquid, its loose-threaded seams

rupture and tear. Calamitous rock
jiggles below, mirrors sway.
Akira, my Japanese student-tenant

is helpless. In Kobe
his family scrambles block to block
seeking shelter. His grandmother cries,

"The smoke, the rubble,
it is like aeroplanes come again."
Akira's poor English, mostly

mathematics and engineering,
leaves us stranded,
unable to communicate how quakes

are measured. Haltingly,
he helps me understand his future,
its doomed oriental certainty.

In the weak economy back home,
his degree worthless,
he will hire on at a brewery

and stay for life.
Only the molten earth
buckling under us promises change.

Finches

This is the season's third clutch
of finches

their purple-throated offspring, little larger
than a child's thumb—

you were careful with the first two.
even as they left the begonia

in tatters, but tonight
without thinking

you pour water into the gullet
of the plant,

hear the wet commotion
of wings

leave unscheduled
watch that awkward

not-quite-flightworthy
tumbling down to grass and brush.

I keep the cat in
overnight.

By morning, stronger,
fledgling wings used to advantage

they have
laddered back.

. . . ask any bat

what it's like to fly
through NYC,
to navigate
those sheer glass
canyons,
high-pitched
signals skittering off
at all angles,
no recognizable
echo, no sonic map,

compare it to
the rough bark
of a tree
faced vertically,
its perfect acoustic mirror.

The Red Knot and the Butterfly: A Fable

The Monarch and the Red Knot
With many miles to go
Had dropped to settle on a rock
Conveniently set low.
Horseshoe Crabs from all around
Clustered in a row.

Said the Monarch to the Red Knot
"For what reason are you here?"
"To gobble up the Horseshoes's eggs,
Enough to last the year.
When fat enough I'll fly away."
"Then why the bitter tears?"

"The time has come," the Red Knot said
"To talk of many things:
Not shoes—or ships—but mostly eggs,
As such I need to sing."
"Alas," the Grandest Horseshoe cried,
"So few of us remain. They think

us a medical advance,
Blue blood that they can drain,
Then cast us back exhausted, weak,
And often leave us lame.
I fear the thought of laying eggs
Seems all the more insane."

"But wait a bit," the Monarch cried
And playing tit for tat,
Asked: "What of me, my milkweed's gone,
How should I grow fat?
The farmers come to spray their grain
And kill all this and that."

"I weep for you," the Red Knot said,
"I deeply sympathize,

But soon you must acknowledge
We don't see eye to eyes.
The milkweed is but of little use
To any such as I,

For I must navigate the earth
Each year from pole to pole
While you make only shorter hops
From everything I'm told.
I must be getting on, my friend,
It's starting to feel cold.

Perhaps I should just change my tastes
And dine on butterflies—"
The Red Knot uttered half in jest.
The Monarch shrugged and sighed,
"You look out only for yourself—
And feel so satisfied."

"You both might think this through a bit,"
The Grandest Horseshoe said,
"And find yourself short-sighted,"
He chided him in red,
"For if milkweed and my eggs are gone,
We *all* could soon be dead."

. . . with the spider lily

there is so much time
        after
the crown of dark green,
spiked leaves
appearing out of season, driven out
from beneath a bed of dead leaves
during the coldest month,
time the bulbs use
to squander what remains from summer, stored away
sequestered in the darkness
        while
the pleasure lies in seeing this lily
stake its claim on winter with its slender leaves
laying over, almost flat, against the ground,
then gone,
no sign of green
        until
months later, when we have forgotten,
        when
the single straws of green erupt
buds swell, buckle open at their crown,
explode, less a flower
        than
some leafless, botanical firework
shooting out its lattice
of red tracers
that curve back onto themselves,

        an entire universe exposed.

III.

Put on the river
like a fleeing coat,
a garment in motion. . .

James Dickey
"Inside the River"

Near Smithfield

I never heard my uncle say:
"This is a working farm,"
though some things, even unsaid,
carry in their silence the weight of words.

My aunt's cactus garden on the sun porch
said it in other ways. So did
the gourds rising on shadowy trellises
foregrounding watermelon and cantaloupe fields.

I remember how the sand swirled
in the dark batter of humus
and that one blind mule we led to the trough
to drink. Our arms ached

from the work the pump did to us.
"The rain is only skin deep," he would say,
"nothing to wet your whistle."
To demonstrate, he would paw

at the damp earth with his foot until a gray talcum
was dislodged from beneath the dark surface.
Tassels of Lilliputian corn withered in the dry wind
that whirled in eddies over the fields,

dust tossed backward over the earth's shoulder
like luckless salt. From the crib
of feed corn, kernels hard as B-B's,
rats stared at us with wet bituminous eyes.

Boundaries

Pacing the wooded lot,
we are touched by different things.
Through a camera's lens I watch for compositions
for lights and darks, for subtle shades,
my temperament suited more to seek
the gradations of color I see in pine sheddings
that carpet our path. Further uphill
you spot a cow's skull in the twisted grass,
your eye transforming this hill,
an imaginary Golgatha covered in forgotten weeds.

The path is wet. Two thin ruts
run through it to a neighbor's field.
Our stand of trees, ready now to harvest,
has been in the family three generations
and again we are touched differently,
your eye projecting how cutting clear
will see these forest acres
dimpled again with seedlings a summer away.

You can tolerate the ruddy clay and ragged brush,
whatever years it takes
until the understory is subdued
by the thrust of towering timber pines,.
wondering which generation,
will map the next cutting over.

Against the forester's advice
I would leave the tallest trees, a spare canopy
to abbreviate the storm, a place for owls
who could hunt what is cut over,
a centering of open spaces
where I could see next year
newer tendrils deer could reach,
a deferral of sorts. I am grateful
for the forest's umbrella-ed air,
rich with its textured scent, summer's honeysuckle

still thick at the pines' sun-margined edges.

A *farm* you would call it, and hand me
the skull, picked clean as china, to carry.
The mountain stands now between us and the sun.
A chill falls. We walk faster. Locating the exact spot,
your ax rings out sharply
to cut a surveyor's stake to mark the corner
once pointed to by an elm, only its stump remaining.
We hurry forward. A rabbit crosses in front of us
as we leave, and in one quick move you scoop an owl's pellet
from the ground into your pocket.

Ice Storm

The wire-falling green lightening
glows through the storm's night
where ice-laden to pure white
the pines snap and fall like gunshots

as if the house were dug in
and part of some brigade. The azaleas
are as disheveled as we are,
stooped under winter's dropped,

unpardonable ancestry. The ice
allows no footprints. When you walked, father,
to elementary school, your child-waist
deep in snow, you saw nothing like this,

the raw-boned winter trees
fallen about the house in morning
like pick-up sticks. Inside
the fire stalled through the un-electric night.

Frozen, black-edged, our tropical houseplants
are two meridians from life.

. . . each year,

mid-June, we catch the fever,
the urge to sail our clumsy catboat.
Hauled out and overturned all winter,
she is as afraid to swim as some hibernating bear,
her mooring lines coiled underneath,
badly crimped. Sharp barnacles,
bleached white as chalk,
are as large as knuckles on her keel
from a single season in the salt. They flake away
under our stiff, iron-bristled brushes and broad blades.
Probed with chisels, her open seams
take grudgingly to lathered strings of caulk.
One at a time the loose-wicked ropes balk,
then wedge tightly between each plank and beam.
A last coat of lead paint dries.
Anchored in the tide,
the wooden bottom slowly swells, seals.
Half-submerged, watertight now,
we can bail her dry, stow whatever gear,
set the heavy canvas,
then, arms aching, back wind the boom
to catch the slight breeze, start downriver.

Transparencies

The three of us marvel at the way the bream gather,
how quickly they rise to the bait that disappears
as fast as we can roll it from fresh bread into doughy balls,
slip it over the barbed hooks,
that short time before their mouths scramble the water
into thrashing eddies.

The house is still unmatched, its small lake,
then beyond that the broad river.
On quiet nights we hear the pond's overflow drip into the culvert,
listen as it flows forty feet to where the tidal currents
slosh back and forth.

When we moved here I was eleven,
enraptured by the glass-clear fingerling eels,
untold numbers swimming a thousand miles from the Sargasso Sea,
then clustering at high tide around the fresh effluent from the lake.
They would fight their way up the drainage pipe,
up the sheer, moss-covered walls of the spillway
simply to inhabit a necessary stage of life here.

The time is too short
When I am both father and son,
when our generations stretch out their limbs and touch one across another.

At night your grandson hears the throttle of trawlers at high tide,
setting, then retrieving gill nets.
In the morning, when the sand lies exposed,
he wades in the ditched-out course the prop-wash left behind.
Angel clams lie exposed in fragile clusters,
their ruffled shells like ruined white wings
out of which life slipped during the night.
Around him their telltale tracks reveal young horseshoe crabs,
some no larger than a thumbnail. They furrow the mud.
We overturn a few with our toes,
each with its gangly feet dragging behind a saw-toothed, prehistoric tail.

That night I came home to tell you
she had died, you fell on your knees beside the bed
and wept that you had wanted to die first.
I never told you how my mother had looked at me
in pain from her pillow, and said: *Let me die,*
how I had sent you home earlier to sleep
before you collapsed, then sat through those long
comatose hours with my brothers and sister
together in the chrome waiting room
until the end. How to still understand everything
as a stage of something else.
This is the poetry to fall back on.

. . . for three summers

we crossed the James on a flimsy Sailfish,
its silvered mast rising above the deck,
scarcely visible ashore above the earth's curve.
Tacking toward Isle of Wight County's
abandoned lighthouse, we looped our bow rope
over its ladder's lowest rung. Poised there on stilts,
brackish water eddying between her stiff legs,
                              rust consumed everything in sight.

Climbing up—inside—barefoot, we had to
tiptoe among the shards of glass and seagull droppings.
From that vantage point, upriver toward Jamestown,
the past returned our glance. We could see
the mothless Mulberry Island that never yielded silk
                              the colonists sought.

You talked to us about those first settlers,
men left companionless, no women for a dozen years,
but by this point you, too,
                    were *companionless..*

High up, peering through the prismed lens,
I could barely catch a glimpse of your home,
seeming to bob up and down among the oddly-raked,
red-and-white buoys. The channel's numbered markings
                    spelled out our lives.

Letting Go

Home, the summer after your death, a steady gale
has culled the un-swept grass clippings
into rotting levees. Already, the house is up for sale.
Sleeping here at night, the water birds
keep me up with their row. My crab net,
freed from its storage, is taller than my son.
Shedding its twelve year sand glaze,
he wields it like a casting rod in the warm sun,
the water licking his ankles. Stalking the wet
air, he flails away at the unwary river,
scratching out stones, dredging up the outgrown armor
of a blue crab, then clumps of seed oysters.
Years ago I would drop the net and recoil
in pain each time in a moment's eye-blink
the razor sharp mother-of-pearl lanced my heel,
my foot, a startled octopus, emptying its red ink
in writhing spirals. It is still numbness first, then feeling.

Sestina for David

Overnight, ice splintered the dry wood, split stone,
    Sprung up cauliflowered crystals in the mud. This morning
The exposed hillface is lathered in sunlight.
    A deepening crevice collects its purchase of sand
And seed gathered by the loose seine of root claws.
    You step carefully over runnels of snowmelt. Your leather

Boots untidy the mud with their rough tracks, your leather
    Jacket half-open. We cross where two apple yards are, and stones
Had been and were moved south and east. The dense claws
    Of trees take hold here. A ringed fire pit is cold in the morning
Where last evening we burned prunings, then smothered them with sand,
    Left the fire dying, embers dancing, and waited for sunlight.

I awoke early to see meteors falling before any sunlight,
    A shower crossing against our window. Your leather
Boots puddle opposite me next to your bed on the sand-
    Scraped floor, dripping along rawhide from wet eyelets onto the stone
Hearth, while the sky's last ember plummeted eastward through the dark morning,
    Extinguishing over the lake under the bear's invisible claws,

The earth's magnetic tugging, drawing it downward. The claw-
    Marks of its passage incinerate its own light,
Dazzling. The moment, flamboyant, postpones the morning.
    The universe flaming down, ashen snow covers the lathered
Hillside silently, lessons for us being in the stone and not the stone,
    The way unknowable grains of sand

Are carried oceanward, deposited there as brine-washed sands
    Covered in detritus—a gull's quill, razor shells, empty claws
Kept in place by a shim of marsh grass. Now the stone
    Enters us. We are its soul entering sunlight
Through an atmosphere begging with promise. The feathered
    North slope ice cracks under our boots. The thaw this morning

Coming with a cascade of slipping ice, debris. Early spring, a morning,
    Exuberant with the scent of pine, spruce. In the river bottom, sand

Is swirled into hollows by spawning trout. Your leather
    Apron shows the splattered fish blood. Bear claws
Have gouged ribbons into the stream's bank. Sunlight
    Falls twice a year here a certain way between the stones,

Where we know, where we understand the day, the morning to plow, to claw
    Up the earth, tilling the sandy soil, scattering seed. Today, before light
You strip the leathery bark from logs to start a fire. Your eyes read the calendar
                                         in the stone.

Landscapes

1.

You offer
a bushel of oysters

to red-gray coals
cover them

with wet burlap
I am wet

with oily
afternoon rain

still dripping
from dense pine

The alyssum, ageratum
are stained

purple with the oyster's
intense Phoenician palette

2.

At night
heat rises

from our bodies
like a squall-drenched

summer road
In the dark

you slide down
over me

your breasts
tap-dance

over the heart's
bone-joist scaffold

The Dolphin

Forty years ago, I watched
the Arctic Circle aboard a passing freighter
cutting its smooth, earth-girding wake
under summer's sea-circling cool north sun.
"Channel fever" sweated us pilotless
through the night North Sea to Bremerhaven,
latter day merchantmen
bearing arms for a cold Hilter-less war,
summer of Lowenbrau, dark, at Odeon's,
courtesy the "retired homosexual" steward.
Billy Rufus, soft in your tennis whites,
touching down, they met you at the dock
to say your uncle had died. While at sea
we taught Roosevelt to read
the sweep hand on his hundred-dollar watch.
So educated, he blew the ship's whistle
for lifeboat drill. Miles from Greenland
swinging in that powerless boat, we were
thirty feet above the North Atlantic
on two pulleyed cables,
still in that warm current, that dark clash of Gulf
and high summer's limitless day
at the Circle's Arctic edge.
In the evening after mess we trolled the freighter's wake,
hook-less, with scraps of garbage
laced to steel wires, feeding dolphins
through the prop's churning wash.
Not all fish, they ignored the sea's night-muddled fog
to hug our lee at dawn,
arching their dorsum through wave crest and trough,
reliable as morning.

September

This month the alphabet-ed storms
parade close-heeled
like dipping pelicans
strung out along the wind-swept dunes.

The swifts
born on our closed damper in June
circle the house
under an almost black sky

clip their own wings and fall like stones
down the flue to their birthplace
add their voices to those already inside
their excited chittering.

Stinging rain crosses the sky laterally
breakers tear up the ocean's planked floor
prehensile gusts
grasp us tightly, shake us loose.

I give a name to the *fear* for all of us—
man, bird, even the groaning live oak
which has been here
done all this many times over.

Soundings

All numbers, the Bay's deep fathoms' contours
map our coffee table under glass
In August we visit father's younger brother,
his cottage on the Chesapeake.

Grandmother, still in her thirties' bathing suit
in the early fifties
braves the cold eye-stinging water
to turn up worn, worm-tunneled clams
pulled by the undertow,
Grandview's obsolete pavilion,
left to its snow cones, sand
and oyster-shell-paved parking lot.

One dune behind the Bay's ocean-open door
my uncle's trim ship's barometer
hurdles downward,
his anemometer purrs on its windowsill
to tell the storm's fortune.

In August I returned
to render this seascape in oils,
its lighthouse, long-scuttled,
west wall falling away,
brick salted over its rock and barnacle jetty.
Still gutty in its disrepute
its spiral staircase rusts openly in the wet air.

At force eight
gale warnings flag our own lives.
Shedding houses like hermit crabs
we toe the gravel bottom
at a different beach
striking sand dollars, starfish.
Dried, bleached and carted inland,
they scrapbook our lives.

Wind

September 23, 1989:

I still feel it. The wind last night
sucked the breath out of me, flung it screaming
over the live oak and limbless pine.
Then the water swelling, some deep voice
sliding up to us, a dark face, its white woolen beard
spilling over us, straining the ballast
that kept our house rooted like a stiff barnacle
to some tether in the sand
My ears still roar like a seashell.

The ominous calm coming next. That calm
without even the random rustle of life,
birds appearing, silent in the dead air.
When the eye came, I walked outside.
There was a hole straight up
through all that darkness, like a tunnel,
starlight like pinhole punctures in a black screen.
I could barely see the pines, stunted, still straight,
but snapped off midway up, all clipped
the same height, bodiless legs
left planted in clay boots. I could see
cuts opened up in hardwoods, limbs broken
from live oaks, shrubs uprooted, scattered, terrifying.

It came back worse than before,
blowing oppositely, humming its tune
differently over the stringed forest. Inside,
when I fell asleep I dreamed my ankle
braceletted by a whirl of rope leaping overboard
after an anchor, dragging me after it,
dreams of fish flying, their silver pancaked scales
covering my eyes, cutting into me like razors.

Then, this morning. Coming out
seeing sailboats piled like cordwood,

battered and strewn over the marsh,
masts stepped vertically yesterday
laying over now, angled north
as if they were still carrying sail,
reduced to sundials marking shadows in the morning sun,
birds blown north, vagrants, wounded, dazed,
Shells everywhere, freshly gutted open,
still slick with gristle or beaten white
and smooth, broken on some rock,
then carried inland, a whelk settled in a cowshed,
a purplish clam in a seaside garden
where chrysanthemums should be in bloom,
with my neighbors empty house half lifted
from its foundation and nesting in spartina grass,
on an ordinary autumn day
        with bright sunshine, mild sea breezes, soft breakers.

IV.

Not enough risk
in the telling or living.
Not enough blood
in the word.

Jim Peterson
"No Bite"

The Heaven of Poets

And those that are hunted
Know this as their life,
Their reward: to walk
Under such trees in full knowledge
Of what is in glory above them. . .
    from James Dickey, "The Heaven of Animals"

[My wish is] to be killed by a bear
and buried without a coffin
on the west bank of the Chattooga,
and seek my Deliverance there.
    —James Dickey

He is here. His eyes closed.
Bloodless, his fingertips
touch the underside of leaf mold,
his body wedged awkwardly
into a hollow between roots,

a great eastern hemlock
in the richest wood,
where past nights
had seen a doe take on the posture
of sleep. Tendrils of sunlight

twist down into the gorge.
If he had been the hunter,
he is now the prey. They come.
For him this could not be the place it is
without them, the wild boar

searching for acorns
who roots open his shallow grave,
the fox, who takes away the grave clothes,
the bear with perfect claws
who opens his belly,

eats first the liver. The crow

taking his eyes.
Buzzards gather,
share among them his strength.
There is no pain.

His translation is downward,
toward the blood root,
into the kingdom of ferns, of mosses,
of small stones,
toward emotions, pre-vertebrate,

those of the snail, the earthworm,
his blindness now that of the cave fish,
the mole, his silence
that of the garter snake,
whose glistening scales the hawk

clutches in flight.
When the river rises in April,
it scatters bits of bone,
frayed pieces of cloth
in the enjambing waters,

his motion now
is the motion of the earth,
of the sun drifting in its galaxy.
He fell, was torn, rises again,
his soul lifted into the sunfields of heaven,

into the Heaven of Poets.

H. R. "Randy" Spencer was born and grew up in coastal Virginia, much of those years in the family home on the James River, a locale recalled in much of his writing. For the last forty-plus years he has lived in central South Carolina, the last thirty of which on a quiet cove on Lake Murray. Kayaking, birding, and cautiously watching deer from his windows form the inspiration for much of this current volume. His summer employment on a freighter in the North Atlantic and his travels through the Pacific Northwest and as far south as Costa Rica appear in other poems. Water—lakes, rivers, oceans, and clouds—as a dominant motif recurs throughout the work.

The author attended the College of William and Mary, followed by Emory University School of Medicine. As a physician he practiced in psychiatric hospitals and clinics in Northern California and South Carolina, working primarily with children until his retirement in 2017. Both very early and toward the end of his career he concentrated his practice on work with severely autistic children.

Taking classes part-time over several years, he received his M.F.A. in Poetry from the University of South Carolina in 2002. His interest in poetry and healing led to work with the South Carolina Humanities Council where he was a leader in the Literature and Medicine program, and his his experiences as physician and teacher are reflected in the core of his writing. Previous publications include chapbooks, *The Failure of Magic* and *What the Body Knows*. He has been included in several anthologies: *The Art of Medicine as Metaphor, A Sense of the Midlands, The Limelight,* and *The South Carolina Collection.* Individual poems have appeared in literary journals, including *Borderlands: Texas Poetry Review, Fall Lines, and Yemassee.* His three-act verse drama, *Becoming Robert Frost,* has received staged readings and a portion was read in Piccolo Spoleto Festival's Sundown Poetry Series.

The poet is married, with two grown children and grandchildren. He is immensely grateful for the thoughtful criticism and unfailing support from his writing group compatriots: Lisa Hammond, Tara Powell, Tim Conroy, and Debra Daniel. He would be remiss not to acknowledge Jim Peterson, the source of one of the epigraphs, who was his classmate in Jim Dickey's poetry seminar.

CPSIA information can be obtained
at www.ICGtesting.com
Printed in the USA
BVHW031419260319
543749BV00001B/28/P